Thought for th

Acknowledgements

This book would not have been possible without the invaluable encouragement and editorial expertise provided by Tim Pemberton, Managing Editor for BBC Radio Bristol, where these scripts were first broadcast.

I also thank my church Ministers Reverend Brendan Bassett and Associate Minister Reverend Helen Paynter for all their encouragement as I have learned and developed as a writer, and as a Christian.

Most of all I thank my husband and best friend Chris Loxley, who has encouraged and believed in me for almost a quarter of a century.

A third of all net profits from the sale of this book will be donated to Victoria Park Baptist Church in Bristol, England.

www.victoriapark.org.uk

And another third of all net profits from the sale of this book will be donated to "Zacs Place" in Swansea, Wales.

www.exousia.demon.co.uk/content/zacs.htm

Contents

Uncle George

In his prime, my Uncle George was a huge man who could crack walnuts with his bare hands and juggle three children in the air at once.

Aged 90, he's lived through some interesting times, so I've encouraged him to write his life story. "I've spent my whole life avoiding any responsibility or commitment, who'd be interested in that?" he said.

I think it would make a great self-help book.

Like lots of people his age, my uncle doesn't trust banks or dentists. He's more likely to stuff his money in his mattress than put it in a bank.

I grew up hearing his latest accounts of how he pulled his own teeth out with pliers. Once he recounted how he'd tied the end of a piece of string to a tooth and the other end to a doorknob, then slammed the door. His tooth came out whole then he dropped to his knees and almost passed out with the pain and shock. He found this very funny. So did my parents and I, which is very disturbing.

An old Aunt of mine also had a deep distrust of banks. After she died, relatives found her modest life savings hidden in biscuit tins.

Looking at the current global financial crisis and the state of my own endowment policy, I think my Aunt and Uncle weren't so crazy after all. Had I put this money into mattresses and biscuit tins I'd be far wealthier.

God's wisdom can also appear like foolishness to me. As a child I heard bible stories of how God sent a puny boy with a slingshot to kill Goliath the invincible giant, and then crowned him King David of Israel.

Christians believe God loves to collect the lowly like trophies and make them into kings.

400ᵗʰ Anniversary of the King James Bible

Some bible scholars believe that Jesus grew up in a very poor area of Israel. His accent would have been working class even despised. So to celebrate the 400th anniversary of the translation of the Bible into English, my church is inviting volunteers from our diverse congregation to give readings in a variety of accents from across the UK and the world.

The New Testament was written in the street language of ordinary people, not "Posh" Greek.

Although strange to hear now, the language of Thee and Thou in the 400-year-old King James Version was actually the common language of the day too.

I'm reading Isaiah 61 in Bristolian. I love this passage. It's about social justice, and everyday life.

"I, God, love justice, fair dealing and I hate robbery."

Its still relevant thousands of years later, as we witness the rich getting richer off the backs of the poor, alongside the arrogance of those bankers still taking huge bonuses, whilst austerity measures to finance the bank bailouts impact upon the most needy across the world.

Jesus quoted from Isaiah 61. It was his mission statement.

"Preach good news to the poor.
Proclaim freedom for the prisoners (your prison maybe loneliness, addiction, hatred)
Release the oppressed.
Comfort all who mourn
Bind up the broken hearted."

Being a Christian doesn't make you any better than anyone else. It's a journey, where with God's help you try to behave better today than you did yesterday. And when you inevitably mess up, you learn to love and forgive yourself and others, then continue walking. A simple message, but a hugely challenging way of life to put into practice.

Honesty.

I recently went to a street market with my mother. To my delight I found a stall selling my favourite fair trade hippy clothes.

"Will extra lard fit me?" I asked the stallholders, "I'm a big size 16."

"Julie, why don't you just admit it and say you're a size 18?" My mother interrupted loudly.

The stallholder cut the heavy silence by saying, "Yes, look they pull out really wide. I'm sure extra large will fit you. I'm a big size 10, and small fits me!"

"And actually I'm just an enormous size zero," I said, handing over 20 quid.

Shopping with my friend Pat didn't make me feel much better either.

After my father died, my mother had given me the contents of his drinks cabinet. "For all your wild parties," she said.

Pat seems to have no qualms about mixing her faith with spirits and is an expert on how to make cocktails from Contreau and anything in a bottle with a label in a foreign language. Dad had left me lots of these. So we decided to hold a party, and went trawling for cocktail dresses in charity shops. "Oh, Julie look…you'd look lovely in that if you lost two stone…"

The paramedics did a great job on Pat that day.

Christians believe that there are times, when telling people unpleasant truths is in the best interests of those we love. It may hurt. But we must do it if we care about someone and the consequences of the choices they make.

Therefore, not everyone who tells you what they know you want to hear is your ally, and not everyone that challenges or disagrees with you is your enemy.

Christmas Clean.

We usually only tidy our house if we are expecting visitors, which is why I don't like surprises. In winter we usually keep just the front room tidy and herd all unexpected guests inside. We don't leave people waiting at our door in the cold whilst we gather up all our muddles and throw them behind the armchair before letting them in.

So being masochists my husband and I invited both our families over Christmas & New Year. Thus requiring a belated spring clean of the whole house.

On the first day of operation Christmas clean, I shredded one pair of curtains and shrank another pair in the washing machine. That mistake cost me 100 quid.

Whilst hovering I managed to break the Dyson, but after spending several hours bent double hovering with only the upholstery attachment working, I discovered the main hose had broken and managed to fix it with tape. Unfortunately I didn't notice I'd cut my thumb until I was hanging more clean curtains.

After asking God's forgiveness for an outburst in Anglo Saxon, I decided crying whilst eating three helpings of apple pie would make me more productive. It did; I found a cheap package holiday to Tenerife next Christmas on-line. God is good.

My husband and I scheduled a walk after Christmas lunch; alone… In the park, no one can hear you scream…

I have reflected on this craziness of the Christmas and New Year Season. It's not about whether my house is clean enough, or my cooking is good enough. It's about spending time with people, especially lonely, prickly people with broken hearts. Just as God made himself human, came down from heaven to spend time with us. Christians believe that our behaviour should mimic Jesus'.

The Les Dawson Quintet.

Against my better judgment the leader of our church music group convinced me to start playing my flute.

"But I haven't played for 20 years and when I did, I had no discipline and rarely practiced."

"Oh no one notices our mistakes when we're playing in a group. You'll be surprised... Try it."

My first gig was at a baby's dedication service (its like a Christening). I usually hide behind everybody else, but couldn't get to the back of the group in time, so an attack of nerves caused me to play worse than ever. I was mortified I had ruined the family's chosen music... That was until a relative thanked me for playing.

"Wow, they really can't hear our mistakes." I thought.

Then Reverend Brendan decided to resurrect his clarinet from his distant school days. A clarinet is a reed instrument prone to high pitch squeaking in the hands of anyone less talented than Acker Bilk. Once Brendan played a whole hymn without even noticing his sheet music was in a different key to the rest of us. We sounded like a bunch of fighting Tomcats. The congregation sang on regardless. Are they too polite to notice? I wondered... Not this time.

"It's a pity Brendan had to accompany you," remarked Fred, my favourite grumpy old pensioner.

For revenge, I've decided to learn the bagpipes. They sound even worse than a violin in the hands of a novice.

Christians believe God loves to see his children play together. Whether we are virtuosos or novices, God sees beyond outward appearances and looks at our hearts. He judges us on how we use the talent that we do have to help others. If our motives are genuine we sound beautiful to God, no matter what the world thinks of us.

Bunion

I recently purchased some rather expensive mail order shoes to support a painful collapsed arch caused by a hereditary bunion for which I blame my mother. The shoes arrived with a voucher for £40 off a case of wine.

"What a marvellous way to recoup some expenditure on my shoes." I thought.

It was even more marvellous when I discovered that if we didn't like the wine, they'd give us our money back. My husband and I ordered a case and penned a return letter in an attempt to keep the wine and get our money back.

Dear Sir/ Madam,

Thank you for the case of 12 assorted wines. We tried them all and are writing to say we did not like them and they made us ill. Certainly the eighth bottle made us so queasy that we vomited so much we could barely finish the remaining four bottles on the same evening.

Furthermore, the next day we blame the wine for making us feel even worse. It induced migraines, vomiting and acute diarrhoea. We also discovered a collection of bedraggled people sleeping on our lounge floor, who all claimed to be our best friends and that we had told them that we loved them the previous evening.

If this is what your wine does to us within twelve hours of purchase, then your product is faulty and we respectfully request our money back.

Yours sincerely,

Mr & Mrs Loxley

"Very amusing," they replied - But no refund.

Our consciences tell us that returning used goods, which we claim to dislike (even with the tags still attached) is still dishonest. It made me realise that deceit often requires forward planning. It is usually intentional, rather than a result of opportunist temptation.

Texas State Trooper.

Once I rode a 1450cc Harley Davidson 3,000 miles around Texas - two up for charity.

Accustomed as I was to doing ninety on UK motorways I took the same approach in Texas. We had a lot of miles to cover. One day whilst speeding down a deserted highway I spotted a State Trooper driving in the opposite direction. He promptly did a Starsky and Hutch U-turn across the grassy central reservation and made chase.

"Do you think he's after us?" I yelled to my pillion.

"Yes, he's after us. Pull over."

We spent a happy few minutes discussing the weather, which hadn't changed in months. Then he informed me that the speed limit in Texas was 70.

"Oh really Officer?" (*innocently*)

But as I was foreign he couldn't just give me a ticket. And it being a public holiday meant the courts were closed, so he'd have to throw me in jail.

I had visions of meeting 'the sisters' in The Shawshank Redemption.

Luckily, he decided to just give me a warning instead.

I never worked out if he was joking, and I didn't push my luck by asking. Maybe I missed something when I was distracted by his tight thigh hugging pants?

"Yeah, so much so that you didn't notice his rotten teeth." remarked my pillion.

Christians believe that Jesus didn't abolish the requirement for us to obey the law. Jesus said, loving your neighbour as yourself and loving God with all your heart, mind and soul sums up the law. By doing this, we'll satisfy all legal requirements and more. However, I believe God knows how impossible it is for us to be this good. So he gives us his spirit on this journey of life to help us make the right choices.

Beach Party

During my misspent younger days some friends and I organised a beach party. If it *was* slightly illegal at the time, the police never found us. Neither did half the people we invited. Some spent the night alone shivering in their cars.

We had a great sound system and a transit van full of firewood. There were folk who claimed to have known Jim Morrison; it was nice to pretend to believe their stories. It was our own Woodstock, but without the naked dancing hippies because it was too cold in those days when we still had traditional British Summer times.

During the darkest hours of the morning, when the music and fire had died down, a bored biker decided to take a ride up the beach. We heard the drone of his engine fade into the distance then a loud thud, followed immediately by his engine cutting out.

Momentarily, concern flickered through our collective-consciousness...until we heard his many attempts to restart his engine before it fired up. So we knew he'd survived. He returned to the fire to tell us his story. In the darkness, he'd rode into the only upright wooden post on the beach for miles.

We responded with howls of laughter and absolutely no sympathy at all.

Christians believe that God lights our path a few steps at a time. Faith is trusting and believing when we cannot see very far ahead. We learn to live, not in the past with its regrets nor in the future with its fears, but in the present. It doesn't stop bad things happening to us, but I believe God will work some good for us into even our most difficult circumstances if we ask him.

Creator God.

Still travel sick for Alaska, my husband and I visited an English art gallery for the first time in over a year. We saw two paintings, which triggered our glacial memories of Alaska. The razor edged beauty of the ice had been captured in a way that only an artist who had been up close to a glacier could do.

Her views of the Cosmos, also inspired us, like I imagined prehistoric man must have been when he looked up at a night sky unblemished by light pollution. It was so reminiscent of the clear expanse we had witnessed whilst camping 8,000 feet above sea level in Yellowstone Park.

In contrast, Denver and Sydney art museums had large collections of modern art, which we'd struggled unsuccessfully to appreciate, whilst the queue for the Monet exhibition had grown like a 1930s breadline.

When has a Da Vinci or a Botticelli required 500 typed words of explanation so that the on-looker "gets it"? We wondered.

In Sydney, a dismantled escalator drew quite a crowd. It took ten minutes of debate before people realised it was not an exhibit. Some art that we saw, however, did have some useful function. It made us belly laugh uncontrollably, and had made some people very rich.

Christians believe that we were created in the image of God. Therefore, it's no surprise that we have a desire to create too. But does Art have to be beautiful? I believe God made warthogs as well as beautiful mountains, both heroes and ordinary folk. Just because *we* don't understand something's purpose, or appreciate its beauty, doesn't mean it doesn't have value, and isn't equally loved by God.

Mid-Life Budget Camper Van Experience.

During our middle age gap year, my husband and I spent two months in Australia. Being budget travellers we picked the cheapest campervan company in OZ.

Checking the website we saw that they were used mostly by young backpackers. The vans were brightly painted, some with very naughty slogans. So when we booked our van we explained that we were middle aged and could we reserve something conservative like the one with the Rolling Stones mural?

"Oh no, you can't chose your design, but I'll write a note saying you don't want something really "out there"", laughed the wicked lady at Wicked Campers.

The van they gave us came equipped with pink fluffy handcuffs and a feather boa, with explicit slogans plastered across the windows. The "fully equipped" kitchen on the other hand, wasn't.

The next day I emailed the campervan company, "I've handcuffed my husband naked to the steering wheel, then realised you haven't supplied the keys. Should I phone your roadside assistance as technically he can still drive if I change gear? But we're worried in case it's illegal to drive naked in Oz?"

They replied that it was positively encouraged to drive naked in Australia and they were offering a discount to customers who returned their vans naked. Their depot even boasted a photo gallery of older customers standing proudly by their vans whose birthday suits needed ironing.

The prophet Isaiah said in the bible, that when we clothe and feed the naked, God will hear a nation's prayers. When we act justly, God responds.

So after a weekend in which many thousands of pounds were raised for the poorest across the world through Sport Relief; it's good to know that we are still following the prophet's words in 2012.

Beautiful Beast

It's been a long time since I was inspired by beauty, but recently I went to the M-Shed Museum and saw the World War Two Pegasus rotary engine.

I look up and I stop breathing… I am alive again. It is magnificent. Like nine old British bike engines arranged around a propeller shaft. Gleaming pushrods beside granite grey fins.

"I never knew," I tell the beast, "I never knew you were so beautiful."

"Look, you can press buttons and it lights up as the pistons move inside the barrels… Look, look at this" I tell everyone in the museum.

I want to hear it roar. I want it mounted over my fireplace. I want to take it apart and get covered in oil. I want, I want, I want. And I want it now.

Then I remember the sound of my Triumph Bonneville thunder as I drive under the railway bridge to visit my husband before we were married. I just know the Pegasus will sound a thousand times richer. I *need* to hear this. Where's the button that plays that sound? Why isn't the whole museum reverberating like a concert hall with this orchestra of an engine? Don't they know, without the sound its only half the exhibit?

As a Christian I don't believe that God created the earth in six days, but I don't believe in some elements of Darwin's theory of evolution either, its still after all just another belief system that can't be proven beyond reasonable doubt, just like mine.

I believe in a creative designer. One that puts the desire to create within us. And that desire to create something beautiful like the Pegasus, is for me supernaturally inspired.

Ben Hur

I watched Ben Hur over Easter for the enth time.

It's a story of life-long friendship, which turns to hatred, betrayal and the quest for vengeance, woven alongside the bible story of Jesus' Crucifixion.

Judah Ben Hur's family's life is destroyed by both the betrayal of his best friend and Judah's quest for vengeance. Finally Judah witnesses Jesus' crucifixion, and whilst he hangs beaten and bloody from the cross, Judah hears Jesus ask God to forgive those involved in his death. At that point Judah says, "…And then I felt his voice take the sword out of my hand."

After Nelson Mandela became South African President, he also decided the country needed the healing balm of forgiveness more than it needed justice to be served. So white police and army officers who both confessed their crimes and acknowledged their guilt, were not punished.

At one hearing, a policeman called Van de Broek admitted shooting and burning a woman's eighteen-year-old son and then returning to tie up her husband and ignite petrol over him whilst making her watch him die.

The elderly widow was asked by the Judge what she wanted from the policeman. She explained, that he had taken her family, but she still had a lot of love to give. "Twice a month I would like him to visit me, so I can be a mother to him. I want him to know he is forgiven by God and I forgive him too. I now want to embrace him so he knows my forgiveness is real. As she walked towards Van de Broek, he fainted, overwhelmed, whilst some in the court room spontaneously sang "Amazing Grace"

Christians believe that Jesus' death gives even mortal real-life people like us the power to forgive and forfeit our quest for revenge.

Farrold

My parents' first language was Bristolian. I don't think they ever really had much interest in speaking English. My childhood was filled with beautiful phrases like: - Theez cassunt/ bissunt/ assunt and verbs were never conjugated - that was something that only modern married couples did.

"Farrold" is another weird word of theirs. That's like Harold, but with an "F" and double the "Rs" in it.

"Farrold" means "forehead"in English.

My university Education helped me to become fluent in English, but one of my earliest memories of Infant school was asking my teacher how to spell "farrold" she didn't have the faintest idea what I was talking about and I couldn't make the poor woman understand. *She* was obviously not bilingual in Bristolian and English.

Years later a friend took me to Glasgow. I wanted to visit the Gorbals, because of its reputation for being like a Glaswegian Bronx and speaking English in a way we southerners can't understand. We spent a hilarious night in a pub with people who sounded like Rab C Nesbit on amphetamines. They'd never heard Bristolian before either. So my friend interpreted for us.

Contrary to popular belief Christians don't believe that God is a white middle class Englishman who speaks like an old Etonian. We all bear his image. And God loves diversity. An old Biker friend of mine believed God was a Black woman, because he met her in the hippie trippy yippie days of the 60s. Interestingly, Christian novelist WM Paul Young also depicted God as a Black woman.

Jesus famously said, "There is plenty of room for you all in my Father's home, in heaven. I am going there to prepare a place for you".

So don't be fooled into thinking that you don't belong.

Fourth of July Celebrations In Alaska.

Once, I celebrated the fourth of July in McCarthy, a small town at the end of a 60-mile white-knuckle ride down a gravel road, in the Alaskan wilderness. Every road sign peppered with bullet holes.

McCarthy looks like the film set of a classic Hollywood western, with its own pack of dogs lazing in the sun. The handwritten sign in its only public toilet reads, *"The window in this restroom is bullet proof for your comfort"*, as sunlight streams through its holes.

The celebrations included a parade of locally 'homemade' floats, followed by silly games, and a BBQ. Celebrations continued all day as the town folk got drunker and drunker and Poker faced tourists watched from the porch of their expensive hotel.

A very tipsy man with a missing front tooth, wearing a Stetson, tipped his hat and offered his condolences, because we English represented the Imperial oppressors.

In the evening the town folk slowly migrated to our campsite for a free firework display. It looked beautiful in the Alaskan twilight against the backdrop of snow capped mountains and John Denver's music. As the firework display ended a fight broke out between two best friends, sending a nearby table flying onto the campfire.

Only the flies would brave the campsite toilet. So I adopted a civic role of directing women to the best places in the forest to wee.

When I told my Texan friend where we'd celebrated the 4th of July, he said "You did what? Alaskans are like Texans gone wild…" And so they were. A wild country needs wild people.

Like Alaska, some Christian writers describe heaven as an untamed "undiscovered country", a beautiful place full of infinite possibilities, to which God gives us glimpses, like rays of light streaming through bullet holes. Something to dream on during this bank holiday.

The Last Boy Scout

CS Lewis said that God often uses the hardships and trials of life to propel us back into relationship with each other, because we often don't respond to more gentle ways of helping us to get along.

I had this experience recently when an old friend of thirty years disappeared during a motorcycle trip to a bike rally in Germany. The Police came to our door to enquire if this behaviour was out of character for him, as he'd not responded to calls or texts, nor met up with his friends as arranged. We assured the Police that his holidays were planned with military precision.

"He's the last boy scout," we said.

Then for the first time in five years I found myself speaking to his wife. We'd been close friends for decades then we had abruptly stopped speaking over a joke that wasn't funny. Suddenly I was discussing lending her my car or driving her to Dover to identify a body or bring home the injured father of her children. Suddenly our five-year silence didn't matter.

We joked like old times – about having to explain to the Police about their friendly marital separation, whilst still living together. You can't hide anything at times like this we agreed. We could all be prime suspects. After all, she was currently having a new patio laid.

Later that night our friend finally arrived at the bike rally. His wife called and told us that he'd got lost on the German autobahn and his phone didn't work in Europe. We replied that once he was safely home and he'd told his story, we were going to kill him.

For me, God had once again worked good things out of a bad situation in my life. A relationship restored out of an old friend's disappearance.

Judgement.

I've learned not to buy glue or paint stripper wearing my bike gear or anything remotely hippyish. Appearance matters when shopping.

I was surprised however, to discover recently that this dress code also mattered when I tried to buy anal suppositories from a supermarket pharmacy.

I'd made the mistake of wearing my rainbow fleece.

"What are you using them for?" asked the assistant loudly.

Surely that was obvious I thought?

"Constipation", I whispered.

"How often do you use them?" She barked at me.

"Is there a problem serving me?" I replied nervously, praying I didn't meet anyone I knew.

"Yes", she said accusingly, narrowing her eyes, pursing her lips and staring at my rainbow fleece, "*Some* people abuse them."

"How ever do you abuse a glycerine suppository?" I asked.

She refused to answer, lest she became an accessory to suppository crime, but reluctantly handed them over.

I couldn't wait to get them home. First I tried sticking them in my ears and up my nose, but a 4-gram adult suppository just wouldn't fit. When I used force they just bent. And they were too big to swallow. Note to self - must remember to buy children's next time.

Then I wrapped one in a Rizzla cigarette paper and tried to set fire to it. It melted the glycerine slightly before going out. The black smoke smelled too awful to inhale. I must Google "suppository abuse" later I thought.

Jesus also knew what it was like to be judged wrongly, because of his long hair, his beard, his dark skin, his poverty, his working class accent and religion. Jesus understands what its like to be an outsider. He stood in front of people who wrongly judged his motives.

Environmental Armageddon.

Just after I'd spring cleaned, bought a new sofa, and hung beautiful new curtains, my husband decided it was time to tear up the lounge to install under floor heating to run off our solar panels in preparation for environmental Armageddon, the collapse of the world economy and the end of fossil fuels.

I arrived home from work to find books and dismantled furniture piled up in the front room, my new curtains in a heap, floorboards piled in the back garden, and bits of bitumen floor tiles all over the remaining floors.

My new poufy had arrived that day. It was plonked upside down like a cherry on top of a pile of *stuff*.

My friend Lisa said, "Have you seen that film 'The Road'? He needs to build a bunker in the back garden, so we can all come and live with you when it kicks off."

"You can all live with us after Armageddon" I said "If I can live with you now. I can't stand the mess."

We also agreed we'd start eating each other in order of eldest first to save her children.

"We'll be able to help people," my husband said, "When the electricity is cut off. We can warm babies' milk in the microwave and let people do laundry in our house."

"Thousands of pounds on solar panels so we can warm babies' milk in a microwave and have clean underwear, whilst everyone else is running round trying to eat each other." I thought.

Jesus said, "Do not worry about what you will eat, drink or wear. Life is more than just food, and clothes. Can any one of you by worrying add a single hour to your life? So do not worry about tomorrow, for tomorrow will worry about itself. Each day has enough trouble of it's own.

Reflections on toilet cleaning...

I've been a volunteer, rather than a professional toilet cleaner for eight months. It's been a revelation to me.

Sometimes I become invisible, ignored as I go about my business like I'm wearing a Clingon cloaking device. I think some people are too frightened to talk me, lest my perceived low status rubs off on them.

I want to wear a sign, which says, "I am a human being."

I'm also amazed at the things people will discard on a toilet floor. I won't go into details in case you're eating breakfast, but you get the picture. Whilst I'm cleaning I think up wording for all sorts of strongly worded signs I'd like to put up, asking that they refrain from doing this.

I often wonder who would design a urinal with a U-bend, without a means of flushing it? Not a toilet cleaner I'm sure. They were *never* consulted.

I once attended a Christian discussion group, to debate the great questions of our faith. One person's definition of a Christian was someone who leaves a public toilet cleaner than they find it.

I'm sure if there had been public toilets in Egypt at the time of the 10 Ten Commandments, this would have been the 11th. "Thou shalt leave a public toilet as clean as you find it."

Jesus of Nazareth said that at the great heavenly banquet, the class structure of this world will be turned upside down. The lowly will be given the most important seats of honour at the table, the choicest food, and wine, whilst someone else cleans the toilets!

Nelson the First Nation Ghost.

We arrived at Prince Rupert, Canada at midnight, tired after a sixteen-hour ferry trip. The info on the website indicated that Prince Rupert was a one horse town, with one main road. All we had to do was follow it straight to the hostel.

After driving around for an hour getting more anxious that we'd be locked out if we ever did find it - we noticed an old man step out from amongst the drunks that were staggering home that night. Chris stopped the car and asked him directions. Next thing we know Nelson had introduced himself and got into the car. He advised us that we may as well take him home on route, as it was easier than trying to explain where the hostel was. I asked him about his accent, because he did not sound Canadian.

"I'm First Nation," he said, "Native Indian. We have our own laws, lawyers and parliament."

My imagination started running wild. I wondered if he would disappear from the back of the car once we arrived at our destination. He did not. He stepped out of the car and shook hands goodbye. Then walked a few steps away before disappearing into thin air.

We stepped inside the hostel and the owner asked if we had managed to find it OK.

"Yes," I said, "An old Indian called Nelson helped us."

The owner just smiled and said Nelson has been helping lost travellers in this town for a very long time.

"Oh really," I replied, "How long?"

"Ever since the gold rush of the 1800s," the owner replied.

There is a supernatural dimension to the world that we can neither prove nor disprove categorically. I believe that eventually life presents us with a choice to make. What will you believe, whose side will you choose?

Dungeness Lighthouse, Washington State.

The USA has many cheap county campsites, which offer large pitches, each with perimeters of bushes and walls offering a level of privacy, unknown in the UK. Each pitch usually has its own campfire ring for cooking and a picnic table large enough to sit six people.

After posting our honesty fee, we drove around the county site by Dungeness lighthouse, in Washington State to find a good pitch. We were surprised to be alone. We quickly pitched our tent. Then I went looking for the toilets, which are usually heated even in summer!

It was dusk. On my walk back, I sensed I was being watched through the overgrown grass as it swayed in the wind, then I had an urgent need to run. I had a chilling feeling that I was being silently stalked by a group of people, but I couldn't see or hear anyone.

I began to run so fast I could feel my heart beating in my throat. The people I was sure were watching me from the waist high grass, ran in parallel, still crouching, getting ready to pounce. I found our tent and dived in, choking for breath, yet knowing the tent wasn't going to save me. I just wanted to be killed somewhere familiar…

Spookily, the next day, I read about an old Indian tribe that had been massacred in the same spot in 1868. The only survivor had been a young pregnant Indian who had been stabbed and beaten with clubs and left for dead. She'd made her way up the five-mile spit to the lighthouse and was taken in by the lighthouse keeper and nursed back to health.

Evil deeds can leave their imprint on a place for generations. God however, says that he will bless the families of those that do good deeds for a thousand generations.

War Stories.

It was 30 years ago that I vividly encountered the impact of war upon a serviceman's life. I was roughly the same age as my friend when he first went to war. Even then I understood that I was learning through someone's personal history.

Back in his room, against a backdrop of Crosby Stills & Nash, I learned the sound of a man crying who is taken back to a time when his young friends were blown up in the vehicle in front of him, their body parts flying. I learned the sound of regret about wasted years trying to blot out the guilt of surviving when others didn't.

Sometimes, the old woman who lived downstairs found him shaking in a corner of the hallway, crying and yelling like he was being shelled. She understood. She'd seen similar long ago and never imagined she'd have to see this again. The war to end all wars they'd told her.

Once whilst listening to my friend, I recalled a story my grandmother told about a veteran reduced to begging in the streets during the 1930s depression with a tin tied around his neck whilst he balanced on crutches. This was his reward after serving in the trenches. Now I wonder if enough has changed? Do we treat the brave men and women who risk their lives and minds for us like heroes? Doing a job most of us couldn't.

I wish I'd had the maturity to have loved and understood my friend better. I wished I'd had the guts to stay with him during his nightmares.

My old friend, you were never just a rank and number, or a government statistic, a piece of collateral damage, to those of us who loved you. You were a human being. Wonderfully made and loved by God.

A Lesson Learned in Goa.

I love it when God teaches me a lesson using his trademark sense of humour.

I once had this experience in Goa, in India. I was staying in a battered old colonial hotel typical of the area. Our on-suite bathroom came with its own resident gecko.

We became quite friendly with one of the hotel waiters who came to work each day on one of the new Royal Enfield motorbikes that were now being assembled in India. We marvelled at how he could transport all the hotel's laundry on his bike in a bundle the size of a bouncy castle.

One morning I noticed whilst breakfasting in the gardens that there was a racist picture painted on the walls.

"Isn't that a swastika?" I asked my husband.

"Yes, it was a sacred symbol in India long before the Nazis adopted it," he informed me.

Later, as our waiter cleared our table, I pointed at the wall and said to him, "The Nazis stole your symbol."

"Yes," he replied with a huge grin on his face, "But you British stole our country!"

We all laughed at my stupidity.

When we sit in judgement of other people, it can often make us blind to our own faults, so much so that we may fail to see that our behaviour is also unacceptable. That's why the Bible teaches us to stop judging others, because none of us is blameless. And that the amount of grace and mercy we show to others, affects what we receive ourselves.

Train Spotting.

Watching the Olympic ceremonies reminded me of Danny Boyle's other work – his film "Train Spotting".

Ewan McGregor plays a heroin addict who reaches the bottom of his addiction, when he retrieves his drugs from the bottom of a filthy public toilet pan. He gets free from his addiction, but then becomes a successful career addict.

For me, the film was a dramatic portrayal of how the career addict and the drug addict have a lot in common. I was profoundly touched by the emptiness of Ewan's life both as a heroin addict and a property agent in London. The futility of chasing the dragon and then chasing money.

Greek philosophers such as Socrates couldn't understand why we would wish to strive for ever more money and possessions. Once we have met our needs such as food, clothing and shelter then we should seize the opportunity to develop our characters, and to find some meaning in life.

Over two thousand years ago Socrates asked the people of Athens, "Why do you care so much to make all the money you can, and to advance your reputation and prestige, while for truth and wisdom and the improvement of your soul you have no care or worry?"

Centuries later, Jesus Christ put this more simply, "What good is it for someone to gain the whole world, and yet lose their very self?"

Watching some of the Olympic athletes being interviewed after competing, I was often struck by their humility, the sacrifices they had made, and their contentment with what they had achieved, in whatever place they came.

For me, they had mastered some basic Greek Philosophy – that, "He who is not content with what he has, would not be content with what he would like to have."

Bad Santa.

Many of us have favourite films that we watch over the festive season year after year.

For me, top of my list has to be "Bad Santa" starring Billy Bob Thornton. It's so full of profanity that the film can't be shown before the 9 'o' clock watershed. It's also hilarious. "Bad Santa" is a drunk and dirty, crude, cruel man who takes a job as a Santa every year and then robs the store he works in.

Santa is a mess and hates himself so much that he attempts suicide. His life is changed when he strikes up an unlikely friendship with a young boy who shows him kindness. As a result Santa does his first unselfish act that he can remember, and he discovers how good it makes him feel to do something to help others. From this tiny seed, his life changes.

I love this film because its redemptive message is the same message of Jesus of Nazareth. That no matter how drunk, dirty, or profane you are, a small act of giving and receiving love has the power to change your life.

So if you are looking back over the festive season, ashamed of the drunk, crude, cruel, profane, childish, way that you think you've behaved, then God can use you. He wants you on his team. He's used prostitutes, drunks, adulterers, spoiled brats and swindlers before. People who've murdered and persecuted his prophets and his son. The Bible is full of people just like this who he's used to lead and even transform a nation. God takes us as we are, not as we think we should be.

Jesus hung out with, loved, and partied with the marginalised, the ashamed, and the broken hearted. He still does in 2013.

Glide Memorial Church, San Francisco

Amongst the poverty in San Francisco, sits Glide Memorial Church. Within a few blocks of shops selling Prada and Gucci: it provides thousands of free meals to the homeless, and love to the disenfranchised.

It's also a place, which Bono and other superstars have called home. I attended a Sunday service and was treated to the most amazing choir, with female soloists who sounded like Aretha Franklin. Glide is also a place where gay and lesbian people are welcomed. Amongst the many self-help groups, they have lesbian, gay and bi-sexual meetings. Gay men even model the Glide official merchandise on stage, the proceeds of which help fund their social outreach programmes. Whilst many churches still argue about 'homosexuality,' Glide loves and accepts these men and women who play a full role within its community. I'm sure that some religious folk are surprised that the roof hasn't fallen in over Glide. The reality is that lives of men and women, gay and straight experiencing poverty, domestic violence, mental illness, addictions and rejection are having their lives transformed by becoming part of a loving community where the rich rub shoulders with the poor. Glide's focus is on loving and accepting one another and leaving the judging to   God.

In a world where not only the media, but the church appears to be obsessed by sexual behaviour, it's noteworthy that Jesus Christ did not once mention homosexuality and had very little to say about human sexual behaviour. He did however, have plenty to say about social justice, our treatment of the poor and marginalized, and how we manage and spend our money.

If we follow Christ's example then we all ought to be less concerned about sexuality and more concerned with understanding and challenging the causes of social injustice.

Dare to Dream

January is the time of the year when like many people I often consider making plans and setting goals for the year ahead. Like many others I've also become pessimistic with age about what I have the power to change and how long my resolve will last, so much so that I may give up or not even bother to start.

This year I've asked myself, how dare I give up dreaming? How dare I be so cynical?

My life would be very different and much harder if my parents had not imagined, and worked for a better life for their children.

I can vote because a woman threw herself under the king's horse. And I've enjoyed many further rights that my mother did not, such as equal pay, and even the basic right to wear trousers to school and work, because of the activism of women during the second wave feminist movement of the 60s and 70s. We *all* stand on the shoulders of those who have dreamt before us.

For me though this exercise cannot be about obtaining "The American Dream," the wish to become one of the world's richest one percent. Its about hoping and trying to play at least some small part in making the lives of the other 99% of this world better.

Thousands of years ago the prophet Isaiah said, "In the last days, God says I will pour out my Spirit on all people. Your sons and daughters will prophesy, your young men will see visions, your old men will dream dreams."

Ghandi and Martin Luther King died for their dreams. But we'll only get to the Promised Land if we *all* dare to dream as part of a community of dreamers, intent on awakening the conscience of the world.

Bob Dylan

I come from a long line of Bob Dylan fans. My cousin even named his daughter Corrina after a Bob Dylan song.

My brother-in-law bought all his albums and his son is also a fan.

It's hard for me to choose my favourite song. I have a scratchy original 45 single of "Positively 4th street" and I love "Like a Rolling Stone". Both are great passionate songs in which Bob pours out his anger towards proud people, but my overall favourite has to be his pacifist song "Masters of War" the lyrics are still relevant today – nothing much has changed in terms of the human misery of those who experience war, or the lines that are peddled to convince the tax payer, the public and the military that we should wage it.

I went to see Bob live over twenty-five years ago. I never thought I'd ever get the chance. I was apprehensive. I'd heard he could be moody – either spectacular or a huge disappointment. "You owe me Bob," I thought, "You owe my family for buying your records and naming their children for you."

Bob walked onto the stage with just his guitar and a harmonica. He was miserable and uncommunicative with his audience. Occasionally he deigned to introduce a song. He wasn't "electric" in that he didn't have a band. I wondered if they'd walked out mid-tour?

I stayed mad at Bob Dylan for over twenty years and didn't buy another album. I eventually forgave him, but not enough to waste my money on another concert ticket!

The bible says that from those who have been given much, much will be expected. Our talents weren't just given to us for our own benefit and enjoyment, but to enrich our world. Growing up, I admit Bob certainly did that for me.

A Day at the County Fair.

Travel isn't all non-stop excitement…

Once we found ourselves in a small town in Montana during its annual fair. We went along anticipating thrilling fair ground rides and an exciting rodeo.

Half an hour later we concluded that we'd seen a more exciting County fair in a 1970s episode of "The Waltons".

Determined to make the best of things we spent a happy hour inspecting pigs, cows, chickens, rabbits and patchwork quilts, whilst drinking homemade lemonade served by a woman who made Victor Meldrew look cheerful.

We left before the rodeo. Instead we decided a trip to the local bar might offer more excitement for the evening and real ale. But it was our day to be disappointed again. There were a handful of locals debating the inequality of the Olympics, because men aren't as scantily clad as women. An elderly local man offered to take his clothes off if the barmaid would do too. Thankfully that deal was never struck.

Another man was so overwhelmed by the day's excitement that he fell asleep before his head hit the bar. We concluded that this was a trusting community.

Back home there are sometimes unpleasant outcomes to a night asleep on a bar. It's a golden opportunity for practical jokers. Someone had half their face painted to look like a woodland creature, whilst another had a lightly micro-waved Cadbury's cream egg slipped down the back of his jeans. It had the desired affect upon waking. He walked backwards out of the bar trying to remember how he ever got so out of control.

As a Christian I was never promised non-stop excitement, but at times my life has been a white-knuckle ride with a God who still surprises me after 23 years, and with people whose love has encouraged and corrected me.

Cousin Bob.

You may have been following some of the stories and documentaries about mixed race people featured during Black History Month on the BBC. My cousin was a "brown baby" too. The illegitimate son of my Aunt and a black US serviceman, posted over here during WWII. At the time they fell in love, mixed race marriage was illegal in most US states. Consequently, they never got permission to marry.

The President was vocal in saying that the US did not want these "brown babies" over there. This meant that in 1945 my family were blessed with keeping the boy who would grow into a kid that it was impossible to dislike. His descendents have also inherited this loveable gene.

Historians say that as a result of the humane treatment experienced by African Americans posted here during WWII, some went onto become key players in the Black Civil Rights movement of the 1960s. Some of them said that they experienced being treated with dignity by the British for the first time in their lives. In a Bristol street fight, British servicemen fought on the side of Black US servicemen, after white US servicemen had refused them entry to a pub. The British were having none of this attempt by the US to impose segregation.

Before we congratulate ourselves too much, my grandmother and my Aunt also had insults hurled at them in the street, because they held the hand of a "brown baby". So did my father.

Now we can't all be great men and women. But the love, dignity and respect that we show another person could result in them discovering the strength to set the world on fire. Our small but significant part in someone else's story makes us all great.

Camilla and My Nephew

My 30-year-old nephew was recently called out to work at Prince Charles' country home, Highgrove House.

Security guards surrounded my Nephew as Camilla Duchess of Cornwall approached him. He greeted her in his usual informal way with an "Alright."

"What are you doing here?" Camilla replied.

"I'm trying to save your husband some money," said my nephew.

Camilla drove off still laughing, whilst the security guards cringed and informed my Nephew that the future King's wife should be addressed as "Ma'am," not "Alright."

I wonder if any VIPs, celebrities or film stars get tired of all this formality? Or do some really think that they are more important, or cleverer, or more attractive than the rest of us, just by accident of birth or occupation?

And for women especially, "Ma'am" seems far more old-fashioned and aloof than the equivalent masculine "Sir."

In Roman times, to foster humility, when victorious Generals paraded through Rome, they had a slave riding in their chariots beside them, repeating into their ears over and over, "You are not a god. You are not a god. You are not a god."

Jesus Christ introduced us to a new informality when talking to our God and creator.

Yahweh, The Great "I am" became our "Abba," which roughly translates into Daddy.

To which I can hear Him reply, "Alright Kid? I *am* a God, but call me Daddy. Its OK with me."

Clash of Cultures.

My late father, drafted at the end of World War II found himself in Egypt. Sometime during his stay, he found himself in a tent in the middle of the desert, an invited dinner guest of an Arab family.

Presented with a plate of sheep's eyes, my father recounted, how it would have been very bad manners not to eat his fill. He also had to belch heartily afterwards to show his appreciation and avoid insulting his host. After a plate of sheep's eyes, my dad said the belching was the easy part.

During my travels years later, having a passion for motorbikes I became the guest of Texas bikers for a charity event. One night after returning to our hosts home at 3 a.m. I managed to lock the bathroom door from the outside, which after a *moderate* amount of Lone Star beer was a little 'inconvenient'. My travelling companion and I debated waking our hosts, but we remembered that they'd told us they were worried we strangers might be weirdoes or serial killers, so they were sleeping with their guns. So we decided to wee on their lawn and leave them a note to apologise.

"Dear hosts,

At 3 a.m. we locked your bathroom door from the <u>outside</u>. We just had to go to the loo on your lawn. If your neighbours saw – our best suggestion is to say that it's an ancient religious ceremony we just must perform the same time every year Greenwich Mean Time."

Jesus clashed with the culture of his day by educating and having friendships with women, cuddling children, and challenging the powerful. He valued the valueless so much, that He made people angry enough to kill him. Integrity rarely comes cheap.

Cool Hand Luke....

I stayed in Fort Stevens, Oregon, the only place on the US Mainland torpedoed by the Japanese in WWII.

The campsite, boasted a 50s American Diner, and free "all you can eat" American pancakes for breakfast.

Unfortunately, the Diner was under renovation. When we complained about the high price of the campsite, they said the price reflected all the facilities it offered, most of which were closed.

To my horror the pancakes were the worst we had ever tasted in the US, but being on a budget we ate there 3 days in a row.

After experiencing a shower, which sprayed most of its water on the ceiling, which ricocheted off and soaked all my clothes hanging outside, I'd had enough. The next day at breakfast I decided to do a "Cool Hand Luke" record attempt at the free "all you can eat pancakes." I was going to get my money's worth if it killed me.

Even the cook was surprised when I went back for seconds, let alone by the time I was on my 15th helping. She watched as my husband fed me pancakes and massaged my stomach, whilst I lay on my back across a picnic table groaning in agony. I think I got my $40 worth.

We all know about being dissatisfied and short changed, the Rolling Stones even sang about it. I've found a deep and complete sense of satisfaction with Christianity where you get three Gods in one: God my Parent whose love and correction develops my character, Jesus my friend with whom I can share all the struggles and joys of being Human, and God the Spirit a supernatural being who showers me in peace and brings healing to my soul.

Correct Bear Conversation.

I recently did some wilderness hiking with my husband in Alaska, where bears are plentiful.

As I am the better shot, I wore the bear spray, on a holster.

In the event of a bear attack I had to spray into the bear's nose and eyes at close proximity. The spray only lasts a few minutes- so it has to be right first time, or you have one angry bear. It also comes with first aid instructions, in case you miss the bear and spray your husband.

Bear attacks are rare and many people escape, because bears don't waste time killing you before they start eating you (butt first).

Apparently if you meet one, you have to talk to them in a low deep voice to relax them, as you slowly back away. Running or screaming can provoke their hunter instinct, and an attack. "Ok, nice bear, relax…I'm not gonna hurt you...don't eat me…eat my husband."

But this only works for black bears, if its a grizzly its different - that's if you can tell a black bear from a grizzly, to know which conversation to have. Black bears can be brown and grizzlies can be black, brown or blonde.

Then there's the conflicting advice about wearing bear bells. Hard to believe, but 8 ft Bears are scared of people – so jangling bells are meant to warn them away. Some Alaskans think bells just announce dinner, so prefer to carry a high calibre handgun.

Christians believe Jesus said not to worry or be afraid. This doesn't stop bad things happening to me, but God has transformed even my bad experiences into something new and good when I've let him. It's so liberating when I don't fret about the future.

Emmanuel.

During a 3,000 mile charity bike ride around Texas a truck pulled across my path.

Two up with luggage on a huge Harley was like riding a building with an engine. As we slid down the road on our skin, I wondered if I'd kill us both.

Days before I'd prayed to God to ask if he would spare a guardian angel for our trip, to fly alongside the bike. Later that same day a Texas biker had given me a brooch, it was an angel riding a Harley. She'd told me that she wanted to give me a guardian angel for our trip.

We did stop sliding without going under the truck, which drove off, leaving us to meet the police. "Were you two wearing your seatbelts ma'am? They asked…

Next morning I rang the local Harley dealer. An hour later 'Emanuel' appeared to collect the Bike. 'Emanuel' means 'God with us'. Emanuel had us back on the road in hours. He didn't even charge labour costs, just parts.

Riding back to the motel my knees and jaw shook with fear. Then I got more scared. I shook and balled my eyes out, wondering how I was going to get back on. Very reassuring for my poor pillion.

We already had pledges of £2,000 so I couldn't give up. So, I rang a Christian biker friend in England and asked him to pray for me. Peace descended. I became calm, and we road another 400 miles that day.

I have learnt not to be astounded by these "spooky" occurrences anymore, because they happen often, but they're always humbling. It reminds me that God cares for us, however unimportant we think we are, God is always with us.

Favourite Films.

Walking around New York recently with my sister, I took her to the parts of the city, which reminded me of my favourite films.

As we walked over steaming subway grills I explained how I imagined the Alien grabbing our ankles then dragging us off to cocoon us as I screamed for Ripley, played by Sigourney Weaver to rescue me.

In central park I showed her the tunnel where Erica Bain, a radio host played by Jodie Foster was mugged, her fiancé killed, and her Alsatian dog stolen in 'The Brave One'. She responded by becoming a vigilante and hunting down their attackers and rescuing her dog.

Walking over Brooklyn Bridge, the familiar sound of a V twin engine reminded me of Arnold Schwarzenegger looking very cool in black leathers and shades, whilst riding a Harley Davidson in 'Terminator 2'.

Police car sirens, reminded me of the first 'Terminator' film, in which Kyle Reece sped to rescue Sarah Connor from 'the Terminator' that had wrecked a whole police precinct trying to kill her. In my opinion Reece uttered some of the most romantic words in film history, "I came across time for you Sarah."

He'd fallen in love with her after seeing just her image on a crumpled old photograph and volunteered to travel back through time to protect her from the Terminator. Thus began the transformation of Sarah from a weak and frightened girl into the legendary mother of the leader of the Human resistance.

Like Kyle Reece in 'The Terminator', Christians believe Jesus Christ also came from outside of our world to transform us... "I came across time for you...I can transform you into the great men and women that I already see you can be today."

Jewish Julie

The truly horrific massacre in Norway was in my thoughts when I wrote this piece; it coincides with a time when I have also recently discovered my Slavic Jewish Ancestry.

I emailed my brothers to suggest we should celebrate with belated bar mitzvahs, I felt a strong need to do something to honour our Jewish ancestors who may have been affected by the holocaust.

So I joined a Jewish Genealogy site. My research was both exciting and horrifying.

I'm still struggling to find words, which describe the feeling in my stomach when I searched lists of people who could be relatives, who were murdered or survived in the holocaust.

My father was drafted in WWII; he also served in India during partition. He'd been raised as a Methodist, but after watching so much killing in the name of God, he only went to church for weddings and funerals after that. My father believed that organised religion was the root of most of the trouble in the world. He didn't see much of God in religion, so he turned his back on it.

Christians believe that Jesus healed the servant of a Roman Centurion, an enemy of the Jews. He healed the ear that was cut off the Roman soldier who had come to arrest him. He preached that we should love our enemies and those we disagree with, not kill them. "Blessed are the peacemakers," he said. The Message is that simple.

I maybe a minority Messianic Jew, like CS Lewis; I believe that Jesus never intended that there should be any doubt about his message or who he said he was.

Outside Appearances.

On a recent trip to New Zealand, my husband and I were eager to participate in all the traditional gap year activities of the young. So we signed up to go abseiling, caving and black water rafting with people half our age.

The first humiliation was the group weigh-in. I noticed that I was only a mere 40 lbs heavier and 5 inches shorter than the pretty young German girl.

The next humiliation was discovering that the only way I could get a full-length wet suit over my calves was to wear one that was 4 sizes too big.

"Won't such a loose suit get waterlogged?" I asked "and pull me under?"
"Oh no," replied the guide, (like he dealt with women's fat calves all the time), "We don't let people drown on this trip."

The caving involved wading through waist deep water. My wetsuit pulled me under at every opportunity. Each time it billowed and filled with gallons of water, pulling me under, I found it impossible to get up again.

"You look drunk," our guide said, as he dragged me up a tenth time.

Next came the rafting. Had these guides ever seen anyone as heavy as us black water rafting, I wondered? We shot along like rockets, crashing into people, overtaking the safe orderly queue on the underwater river.

Unsurprisingly we reached our destination first. Our guide was so excited, "Awesome... wow...did you see Chris? He was so out of control."

After this adventure, I was grateful that whilst Man may look at our outside appearances, God looks at what is in our hearts. He sees through our clumsiness and our ugliness. He sees the apple of his eye. The child he loves.

Red Wine.

My husband and I were recently given a £40 bottle of red wine. We'd never tasted such expensive wine before and we were looking forward to drinking it accompanied by a luxury meal I had purchased especially for the occasion from Marks and Spencer's.

Just as we sat down, our friend Alan who we hadn't seen for months arrived unexpectedly. I was keen to hear all his news and all about his new business venture, but I wasn't keen to share the best wine I'd probably ever drink in my life.

Now Alan is a biker, who I'd only ever seen with a beer in his hand. I reasoned that the likelihood was, if I offered him wine, he'd refuse it, as long as I left out the bit about it being a £40 bottle, as that could spark his curiosity enough that he'd want a glass.

"Wine Alan?" I said as low key as I could make it.

"Oh, no thanks not for me." He replied.

So, whilst my husband and I drank velvety red wine with chocolate undertones, Alan drank tea.

Later in the evening Alan and my husband went down to the garage to discuss their latest projects, leaving me alone with the bottle. So I managed to sneak an extra glass for myself. I could get used to this luxury I thought. And it's amazing my guilt doesn't even affect the taste…at least at first.

Therefore, what is truth I began to wonder? Is it simply not telling lies? Or is being truthful, also about not withholding crucial information that could impact upon the choices people make?

Deceit I discovered becomes easier the more we practice it.

The Good Samaritan

We had a rare experience in Australia. A campsite with shower curtains. Unfortunately it also came with a resident 8-legged monster.

It started towards me just after I'd soaked my hair. With a red hue it looked deadly poisonous. So I let out several blood curdling screams, tripped over the shower tray, and fell face down on the floor as I tried to escape. I grabbed my travel towels, ran out of the shower room, screaming for Chris, my husband...who claimed not to hear me.

"We all heard you scream from the other side of the campsite," said the Aussie Lady running to my rescue.

"I've been sent by the men to find out what's wrong" (Chris thought the men were just scared of the screaming wet woman).

I said, "A big spider, it's got a red hue, I think it might be one of your poisonous ones."

Boy was this woman both brave and professional. She knocked it off the shower curtain with her bare hands and then rammed it down the plughole with a stick.

She and I were quite a sight. And lots of campers stopped to watch. Me wearing dripping wet travel towels the size of fig leaves. She bending over the shower tray, wearing a denim mini skirt, flashing her tattooed muffin tops. I was in awe... These Aussie women are tough.

After thanking her, I resumed my shower and as the adrenalin wore off I realised I'd fractured a toe trying to escape the huge beastie.

After this adventure, I realised that God doesn't always send the helpers we expect. The physically largest and strongest in our society aren't always the bravest. And kindness should not be mistaken for weakness.

Things to do in Denver...

Planning a six-month trip around America was becoming information overload. So my husband and I decided to ditch the guidebooks and use a good beer guide instead. So we navigated by microbreweries.

During a detour to Denver, a friendly barman liked us Brits so much, that he gave us free samples of Wild Turkey whisky chasers with our ale. Yum, my favourite bourbon. Assuming that my sister and husband didn't like theirs, I emptied their glasses into my mouth.

Denver is almost 8,000 feet above sea level. Catching a cab to our motel, I discovered that not only had the Wild Turkey made it through a huge steak into my blood stream, but that also the thin air magnified its effect to the power of 10.

I arrived back in our hotel room in a very jolly mood, and then fell over. Luckily my face broke my fall.

Later during a 2 a.m. toilet trip, I slipped on the bath mat and landed like a capsized turtle in the bath. Luckily, I was still finding everything about the world very funny, unlike my husband. The next day however, I awoke in agony, and remained so, until two days later we found an osteopath in a one-horse town in Colorado. $85 later, he'd repositioned my neck and back.

The bible has many positive references to alcohol, and shows the difference between enjoying a drink and having too much, which I discovered in Denver, is very easy to do....

And church is a place where people like me try to choose to behave better today than they did yesterday. If they let me in, they'll let you in. Jesus didn't come for the righteous. He came for people like us.

Thorn in my side.

If my husband wins the lottery he has no intention of whisking me off to a tropical island paradise, or buying me a flash car.

No, my husband dreams of buying a variety of old furniture lorries and used cars, waiting until everyone goes to work, then parking them up and down the street, in retaliation for never being able to park outside our house, when we have a car full of shopping. He also obsesses about releasing lorry loads of cats into every cat owner's garden whose cats he's convinced have left deposits in his vegetable patches.

Like my husband, a New Testament writer called Paul, also had a thorn in his side. Paul described how he begged God to remove it… Some biblical historians believe the thorn, was in fact his own difficult "Victor Meldrew" type personality, which he wanted God to remove because it didn't win him many friends.

There's no evidence in Paul's writings that God ever relieved him of his thorny personality. Paul literally bored a man to death with his preaching. He fell to his death after falling asleep at an upstairs window during one of Paul's sermons. Without missing a beat, Paul ran down 3 flights of stairs, threw himself on the body and raised him from the dead. The poor chap had only been alive a few seconds, when Paul frog marched him back upstairs so he could listen to the rest of his sermon. Paul continued preaching until dawn with no further casualties reported.

Like Paul, we aren't perfect. We can all be thorny at times. So my thought...indeed prayer for today... is that you and I may lose our Victor Meldrew persona and just be a little less thorny.

Tosca, An Opera by Ernie Wise.

I went to the opera to see Tosca. Reading the blurb, I expected to recognise jingles used for advertising anything from airlines to aftershave. Twas not to be.

Tosca is a tragedy, which made me laugh until my belly ached.

One scene had the Pope sat on a chair on top a platform carried by four pole bearers dressed like the Klu Klux Klan. Reminiscent of one of Dave Alan's religious sketches.

The wonderful diva that played Tosca oozed sexuality. I love opera singers. The women have flesh and curves and breasts, rather than the starved creatures women are expected to be nowadays. However, it was hard to picture this Diva as a Tosca who was described as having a delicate hand and being as lithe as a leopard. I pictured larger jungle animals.

In the final scene Tosca throws herself off the castle ramparts after her lover is shot dead by a firing squad. It looked like this lady threw herself through the crenulations belly first. I thought she was going to bounce back. I had to stuff my fingers in my mouth to stifle my hysterics, whilst I wondered if Ernie Wise had written the script? I only know she wasn't seriously injured because she showed up for the curtain call.

The music and singing were fabulous and as I left the theatre I could hear the opera buffs exclaim what a brilliant production it was. All wasted on a plebe like me who was entertained for all the wrong reasons.

Opera contains strange plots and colourful characters, but the Bible has even more incredible stories of intrigue, infidelity, murder, passion and punishment...but all with a purpose. If you like a good story line, try reading it.

Romantic Fraud.

Years before the advent of the Internet, I was once a victim of romantic fraud.

My husband was living in a shared house when we met. While we were courting I enjoyed many scrumptious dinners there. Wintertime was best. I'd arrive on my motorbike, face frozen in my open face helmet, step inside the house to see Chris stirring a warm pot all ready to serve.

Many months later, Chris moved to a new house. Looking forward to my first dinner invitation, I was disappointed to be served an undercooked Fray Bentos pie with tinned mushy peas. I discovered this was as far as Chris' cooking skills went. All previous delicious dinners had been cooked by his housemate Malcolm.

Apparently when Chris invited me to dinner, when he heard me ring the doorbell he'd pose at the stove stirring a pot whilst Malcolm let me in, so that Chris could claim these creations as his own.

By this time I had a real dilemma. I had agreed to marry Chris, but Malcolm was clearly the culinary expert and I was a foodie that couldn't cook. If I could get Malcolm alone, if I asked, would he be interested in marrying me I wondered?

To my horror, I discovered Malcolm was already betrothed.

Although Chris did have two nice motorbikes…

The ninth commandment says we must not lie. But dishonesty is not just about telling lies. It's about deception, telling half a story to give a false impression in order to manipulate people or situations to our advantage.

We may often see dishonest people prosper. However Christians believe that we should do the right thing regardless of whether we are rewarded for doing so in this life.

About the Writer

Julie Loxley has a degree in Law and a Masters in Human Resource Management. She has travelled throughout North America, including Alaska and Canada. She started broadcasting her 'Thoughts for the Day' on Radio Bristol in 2010. She lives in the South West of England with her husband and their two motorbikes.

8857534R00048

Printed in Great Britain
by Amazon.co.uk, Ltd.,
Marston Gate.